The Heartwarming True Story of a Little Blind Lamb

Peanut
of Blind Faith Farm

Written by Jim Thompson
Illustrated by Rebecca Gavney Driscoll

LITTLE CREEK PRESS®
AND BOOK DESIGN
Mineral Point, Wisconsin USA

Little Creek Press®
A Division of Kristin Mitchell Design, Inc.
5341 Sunny Ridge Road
Mineral Point, Wisconsin 53565

Book Design and Project Coordination: Little Creek Press

Second Printing
October 2017

Printed in Wisconsin, United States of America

For more information, to contact the author, or to order books:
www.blindfaithfarm.com

Library of Congress Control Number: 2017940907

ISBN-10: 1-942586-27-2
ISBN-13: 978-1-942586-27-2

To my wife Laura who instantly saw the opportunity to create an environment for Peanut to learn the skills she would need. If it's true that: *"We can judge the heart of a man by his treatment of animals"* (I. Kant) then truly Laura has a heart of pure gold.

To my children Erika and Michael, your growth and the joy that you share with the people who surround you are a source of great pride. And for your encouragement I am really grateful.

To people everywhere who have rescued an animal from a shelter or from any dire situation, congratulations!

ACKNOWLEDGEMENTS

In memory of my friend of 50+ years, Jim Koch. He lived his life with a dignity and grace (his favorite word, along with "Packers") all his own. He was and still is an inspiration as a friend, and a model for us all as a Christian, husband and father. Thanks Jimbo.

Thanks to my father and mother-in-law, Jack and Sharon Stremick. For giving us Laura, and for teaching a novice hobby farmer how to build pastures, fix a tractor, keep livestock, and for sharing their visions of farming.

To all those,
both animal and human,
who struggle through adversity
to live productive, fulfilling lives.
And in doing so, reward us all.

Farmer Jim woke up on a beautiful summer's morning, eager to start his day. His farm had a flock of sheep with eight new additions! Jim and his wife, Farmer Laura, enjoyed watching the newborn lambs frolic and chase each other all around the pasture.

But there was one lamb that was not participating in the fun. She stayed close to her mother and showed no interest in playing with the other lambs.

"Let's take this little lamb and her mother back to the barn," Jim said to his wife. Laura gathered the tiny lamb in her arms. By the time they arrived in the barn, Laura had decided the lamb should be called Peanut.

Little Peanut bobbed her head in every direction and turned her ears toward the smallest of noises. It was as if she were trying to understand her new world just by listening.

That's when Jim and Laura realized: Peanut was blind.

Jim called the veterinarian, who confirmed that the sweet little lamb was unable to see. "It's hard to imagine how she'll be able to survive," the vet said with a sad shake of his head.

Jim and Laura looked at each other. Then they looked at Peanut. She had dark brown wool with a little curly halo of white on top of her head. "She's so beautiful. Maybe she just needs our help," Laura said. Jim nodded. "We have to try," he agreed.

Thankfully, Peanut had a wonderful mother, named "Sweetie Pie," who was doing a good job of caring for her newborn lamb. Sweetie Pie cleaned her and fed her, which made little Peanut wag her tail just like a puppy.

After eating her first meal, little Peanut looked very tired. The rest of the flock had returned to the barn, and all the other lambs had lain down next to their mothers. Peanut kept standing, but she looked so wobbly that Jim was afraid she might tip over. "Since Peanut can't see the other sheep, I wonder if she needs someone to teach her how to lie down?" asked Laura.

So, Laura went inside Peanut's stall and taught her how to lie down. First she folded her front legs, and then her back legs. It took a few tries, but soon Peanut was lying down just like the other sheep. Tired from standing for so many hours, Peanut nestled into a soft straw bed and fell fast asleep. After that, whenever she was tired, she was able to lie down on her own.

Over the next few days, Peanut explored all the smells and sounds of the barn. Her ears were always twitching and listening. Jim hung a jumbo-size jingle bell around Sweetie Pie's neck, so Peanut would always know where her mother was and could run to her for safety and food. The little lamb grew and grew.

There finally came a day when Peanut was old enough to go out into the pasture again. She had a wonderful time eating the tasty grass and listening to the many wondrous sounds of the outside world.

But Laura was worried. "How is she going to find water when she is unable to see?" she asked.

"We have water buckets along the fence," Jim answered.

"Yes, but how will she ever find them in this big pasture?" his wife wondered.

They didn't have to worry for long. Peanut found the water by sense of smell and touch. She traveled along the fence line until—SPLASH!—she ran into a bucket. She shook the water from her head and drank as much as she wanted.

Then another worry arose: How would Peanut get along with the other sheep?

Sheep like to head-butt each other. It's their way of playing, "talking," and showing who's boss.

One day, a sheep named Stella decided to show she was boss by head-butting Peanut. The head butts were so hard that they knocked Peanut over every time.

"Did you see that?" Laura cried. "We've got to do something."

Jim came up with the idea to divide the flock to separate Peanut and Stella. In the smaller flock, Peanut still received head butts, but they were softer, friendly head butts from more gentle sheep.

Winter came, and there was no more grass. The flock would crowd around the hay feeders for their food. Some of the sheep chased Peanut away, but she was smart. She would stand back and listen. Somehow Peanut knew when there was more room at one of the feeders, and then she would sneak back in to grab her share.

When spring arrived, there was plenty of new grass in the pasture. There were also shade trees in the pasture plus a rock pile and even a few holes. They must have seemed like mountains and canyons to a blind sheep. But they didn't seem to bother Peanut. She often climbed to the top of the rock pile and stood there, listening to all the sounds around her.

There was an apple tree just outside the pasture. Like all the other sheep, Peanut loved apples. With her sharp ears, she was able to hear when an apple hit the ground and quickly hurry over to gobble it down.

One day, Laura plucked an apple from the tree. She called out to Peanut and waited for her to come. Peanut ate the delicious apple and was eager for more. After that, whenever Laura called to Peanut, her ears would perk up and she would always come running.

The springtime also brought new lambs. The newest members of the flock played, chased, and bounced around the sweet green grass. Laura wanted Peanut to join the fun, so she called out to her, "Come on, Peanut! Run!"

Peanut's ears picked up the sound of all the lambs running, so she trotted toward the noise and joined in.

Jim put an arm around his wife's shoulders. "Now isn't *that* a wonderful sight to see," he said as Laura smiled.

As the weeks passed, Peanut showed herself to be one of the smartest sheep in the flock. She couldn't see obstacles like fences, so she began to do something that none of the other sheep did. There was long grass on the other side of the pasture fence, and she put her head through to eat it. Peanut could always be found by looking for a head poked through the fence.

Being around the other sheep made Peanut more confident. Once, while eating near a crabby, old sheep named "Patches," Peanut gave Patches a gentle head butt. Patches looked surprised, but she accepted it as a sign of respect.

As she grew older, Peanut kept learning and changing. When she turned two-years-old, her wool turned the color of vanilla ice cream, just like her mother's. As a three-year-old, she listened carefully for the sound of a gate opening, realizing there might be an apple coming. By then, she was joining in playtime all the time and often was the one to begin it.

Peanut showed the farmer and his wife that a blind sheep can do almost anything. In a short time, she became a respected member of her flock—and the star of what is now called "Blind Faith" farm.

MORE ABOUT SHEEP

Sheep have been living among people for thousands of years.

The most commonly used product from sheep is their very special hair, called wool. Wool is very warm. Every year a sheep grows a brand new coat, called a "fleece." On very big sheep, one fleece can weigh over 15 pounds!

Male sheep are called rams and females are called ewes, and very young sheep are called lambs.

Some sheep breeds are very small (smaller than a poodle dog) and some sheep are very large and can weigh 350 pounds!

Sheep like to be together in groups called flocks.

Sheep really dislike being alone and will often cry and holler (called a "baa" or a "bleat") until they are brought back together with their flock.

Sheep have excellent hearing and their big eyes gives them the ability to almost see all the way behind their head.

Sheep prefer to follow a leader when going into a new place.

Sheep are very tuned into where they live and are experts at staying out of trouble!

Sheep are grazers, which means they prefer to eat different kinds of grasses which they nip off with their lower teeth. Sheep do not have top teeth in front. They pinch the grass between their bottom teeth and a pad that is on the top.

There are more sheep in the world than any other farm or ranch animal.

If you would like learn more, please visit us at:
www.blindfaithfarm.com

ABOUT THE AUTHOR

Jim Thompson and his wife Laura, live on a hobby farm in Jefferson County, Wisconsin. An Air Force veteran, Jim returned to Wisconsin in 1983, and graduated from the University of Wisconsin-Milwaukee with a degree in Zoology. He spent the next 20 years with the Wisconsin Department of Natural Resources, mostly as a Lake Michigan Fisheries Technician. Semi-retiring in 2007, he "took up hobby farming." Not long after, he and Laura acquired five Shetland sheep as an experiment, to help keep the farm's vegetation under control, with thoughts of also producing fine Shetland wool for Laura's knitting and spinning hobbies. The flock of five soon turned to 15; including a tiny blind lamb named Peanut, who inspired Jim and Laura to name their property Blind Faith Farm. The farm produces mostly Shetland wool and Blind Faith's fleeces have garnered numerous awards. Jim has two children, Erika, a teacher in Homer, Alaska and Michael a biomedical technician at Children's Hospital in Milwaukee. Aside from tending to farm chores, his other pursuits include fishing but rarely catching, and admiring whitetail deer. The rest of his spare time is spent planning his next trip to Alaska, researching the perfect grilled halibut or salmon recipe, and just hanging out doing anything with Michael.

ABOUT THE ILLUSTRATOR

Rebecca Gavney Driscoll is a professional illustrator residing in Wisconsin. Her love of nature inspired her to start depicting the world around her at a very young age.

She studied art in the UW-Wisconsin system and works with various publishers, creating greeting cards and illustrations for children's books. Rebecca's favorite subject is illustrating animals and her favorite medium is watercolor as she loves the feel of the paint. Rebecca is also experienced with computer illustration tools such as Photoshop.

Rebecca lives with her husband Dan, a sheltie named Cricket and a cat named Mopsy. When she isn't drawing nature, she is gardening in her yard and at her local Rotary gardens where her artwork adorns the gift shop.

You can see more of Rebecca's work at www.rgavneydriscoll.com. She also adores working on tree and plant illustrations and you can see some of that art at: www.etsy.com/shop/Rgavneydriscollart